Zen Kittens

MEDITATIONS FOR THE WISE MINDS OF KITTEN LOVERS

Buddha
and the editors of
Mango Media

Published by Mango Media Inc.

All Design and Layout: Roberto Núñez

ISBN 978-1-63353-523-7

"I don't want to convert people to Buddhism. All major religions, when understood properly, have the same potential for good."

Tenzin Gyatso, the 14th Dalai Lama

TABLE OF CONTENTS

MIND AND BODY 9

Verse 1: "The body is a Bodhi tree... " 11
Verse 2: "Let him be able, and... " 12
Verse 3: "Beware of the anger of the... " 13
Verse 4: "Having abandoned sensuality—mindful, alert—don't consort... " 14
Verse 5: "Careful amidst the careless, amongst... 15
Verse 6: "Any kind of material form whatever... " 17
Verse 7: "As rain breaks through an ill... " 18
Verse 8: "The 'thusness' of the mind,... " 19
Verse 9: "As the fletcher whittles anstraight his... " 20
Verse 10: "Therefore, the man who seeks... " 21
Verse 11: "Speak or act with an impure... " 23
Verse 12: "Fine words bear fruit in a... " 24
Verse 13: "In making efforts to overcome wrong... " 25
Verse 14: "Understand that the body is merely... " 26
Verse 15: "Free from passion and desire,... " 27
Verse 16: "Having torn one's fetters asunder... " 29
Verse 17: "By your own efforts waken yourself... " 30
Verse 18: "However many holy words you read... " 31
Verse 19: "Do what you have to do... " 32
Verse 20: "All that we are arises with... " 33
Verse 21: "Awake. Be the witness of... " 35
Verse 22: "But when he perceives the disappearance... " 36
Verse 23: "Let a wise man blow off... " 37
Verse 24: "And how does one, in... " 39

HAPPINESS 41

Verse 25: "There is happiness in life,... " 42
Verse 26: "He who is earnest and meditative... " 43
Verse 27: "If a man speaks or acts... " 44
Verse 28: "Happiness or sorrow: whatever befalls... " 45

Verse 29: "Give thanks for what had been... " 47
Verse 30: "It is in the nature of... " 48
Verse 31: "Whether touched by happiness or sorrow... " 49
Verse 32: "There is pleasure and there is... " 50
Verse 33: "For a while the fool's... " 51
Verse 34: "Can there be joy and laughter... " 53
Verse 35: "Just as water cools both good... " 54
Verse 36: "Pleasant feeling is impermanent, conditioned... 55
Verse 37: "Why do what you will regret... " 56
Verse 38: "If by leaving a small pleasure... " 57
Verse 39: "There is no fire like passion... 59
Verse 40: "Fresh milk takes time to sour... " 60
Verse 41: "Nothing tends toward loss as does... " 61
Verse 42: "Righteousness when well practised brings happiness... " 62
Verse 43: "Cherish the road of peace.... 63
Verse 44: "The virtuous man delights in this... " 65
Verse 45: "I gladden my mind, fill... " 66
Verse 46: "Nothing brings joy as does a... " 67
Verse 47: "Know for yourselves: These are... " 68
Verse 48: "How happy he is following the... " 69

VIRTUE 71

Verse 49: "In all the world, every... " 73
Verse 50: "The perfume of virtue travels against... " 74
Verse 51: "He whose evil deeds are covered... " 75
Verse 52: "Let no one work another one... " 77
Verse 53: "Be quick to do good.... " 78
Verse 54: "The evil done by oneself,... " 79
Verse 55: "Let no man think lightly of... " 80
Verse 56: "Never let them wish each other... " 81
Verse 57: "Quietly consider what is right and... " 83
Verse 58: "Be quiet and loving and fearless... " 84
Verse 59: "Good people shine from afar,... " 85
Verse 60: "If the traveler can find a... " 86
Verse 61: "Abandoning idle chatter, he speaks... " 87
Verse 62: "The friend who is a helpmate... " 89
Verse 63: "Filled with infinite kindness... " 90
Verse 64: "And he who lives a hundred... " 91
Verse 65: "Do not speak harshly to anybody... " 92

Verse 66: "Look not for recognition, but... " 93
Verse 67: "You are the lamp to lighten... " 95
Verse 68: "Life is hard for the man... " 96
Verse 69: "Knowing that the other person is... " 97
Verse 70: "The disciple will find out the... " 98
Verse 71: "Can you hide from your own... " 99
Verse 72: "Well-makers lead the water;... " 101

TRUTH 103

Verse 74: "When seeing your own nature it... " 104
Verse 75: "The wise person drives out heedlessness... " 105
Verse 76: "In every trial, let understanding... " 106
Verse 77: "Your worst enemy cannot harm you... " 107
Verse 78: "Men, driven by fear,... " 109
Verse 79: "By watching and working, the... " 110
Verse 80: "Few are there among men who... " 111
Verse 81: "In one truth is all truth... " 112
Verse 82: "See the false as false,... " 113
Verse 83: "The wise man tells you where... " 115
Verse 84: "Do not follow the evil law... " 116
Verse 85: "Let him resolve upon this mindfulness... " 117
Verse 86: "How can a troubled mind understand... " 118
Verse 87: "Develop your concentration: for he... " 119
Verse 88: "The master finds freedom from desire... " 121
Verse 89: "Do not look for bad company... " 122
Verse 90: "Master your words. Let them... " 123
Verse 91: "The wise have mastered body,... " 124
Verse 92: "Do not carry with you your... " 125
Verse 93: "So was my past existence at... " 127
Verse 94: "Wisdom is purified by morality,... " 128
Verse 95: "No one saves us but ourselves... " 129
Verse 96: "The greatest impurity is ignorance.... " 130
Verse 97: "In overcoming wrong action with attentive... " 131

ETERNITY

Verse 98: "All day long you seek fields... " 134
Verse 99: "Give up the old ways -... " 135
Verse 100: "To share happiness and to have... " 136
Verse 101: "Open are the doors to the... " 137
Verse 102: "When one understands that corporeality,... " 139
Verse 103: "When one sees it thus as... " 140
Verse 104: "Faith is the best wealth for... " 141
Verse 105: "The extinction of greed, the... " 142
Verse 106: "Long is the night to him... " 143
Verse 107: "This is deathless, the liberation... " 145
Verse 108: "In a world become blind,... " 146
Verse 109: "You too shall pass away.... " 147
Verse 110: "Even death is not to be... " 148
Verse 111: "For great is the harvest in... " 149
Verse 112: "Cross over to the father shore... " 151
Verse 113: "When you have understood the destruction... " 152
Verse 114: "Wakefulness is the way to life... " 153
Verse 115: "There is no suffering for him... " 154
Verse 116: "Better than a hundred years of... " 155
Verse 117: "Yielding like the earth, Joyous... " 157
Verse 118: "Let go of anger. Let... " 158
Verse 119: "And he who lives a hundred... " 159
Verse 120: "Free yourself from attachment. Know... " 160
Verse 121: "When your light shines without impurity... " 161

Credits 162

MIND

AND

BODY

VERSE 1

The body is a Bodhi tree,
The mind like a bright mirror
stand. Time and again brush it
clean, And let no dust alight.

We need to maintain our physical health and mental abilities to keep them at their best.

VERSE 2

Let him be able, and upright and straight, easy to speak to, gentle, and not proud.

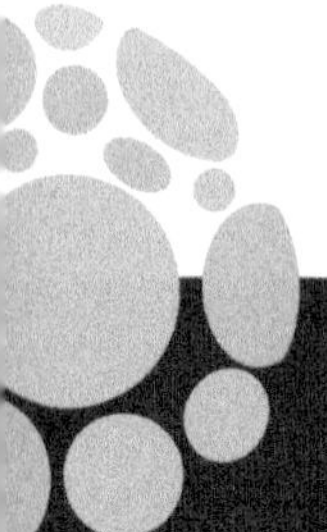

The best things we can be are useful and modest.

VERSE 3

Beware of the anger of the body. Master the body. Let it serve truth.

Our anger is visceral, physical. We must control these impulses.

VERSE 4

Having abandoned sensuality—
mindful, alert—don't consort with
suffering & stress

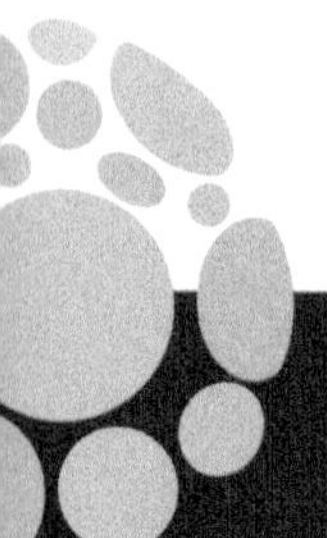

Do not obsess over physical pleasure or pain.

VERSE 5

Careful amidst the careless, amongst the sleeping wide-awake, the intelligent man leaves them all behind

Not everyone understands how to live mindfully. We must accept them as they are and focus on cultivating our selves.

VERSE 6

Any kind of material form whatever, whether past, future, or present, internal or external, gross or subtle, inferior or superior, far or near, all material form should be seen as it actually is with proper wisdom thus: 'This is not mine, this I am not, this is not my self.

Anything that can be taken away from you, even your body, doesn't define you. You are what is inside: your mind, heart, and spirit.

VERSE 7

As rain breaks through an ill-thatched house, passion will break through an unreflecting mind.

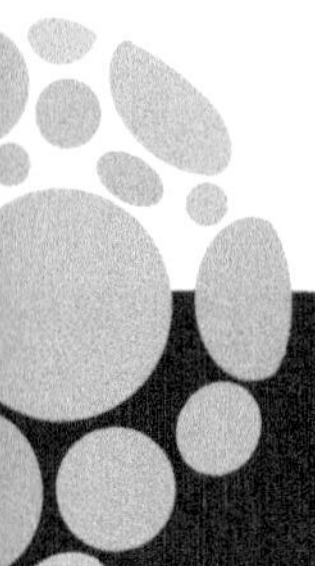

We must train ourselves to resist the influence of bad habits and negative thoughts that would break us.

VERSE 8

The 'thusness' of the mind, just that is true reality.

Our self is at the heart of our experiences, so strive to keep the mind pure and strong.

VERSE 9

As the fletcher whittles and makes straight his arrows, so the master directs his straying thoughts.

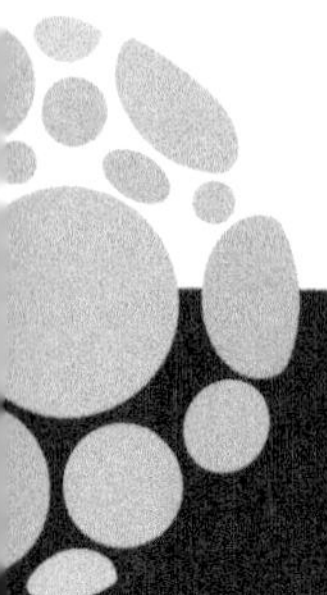

Sometimes, our thoughts and emotions feel beyond our control. Remember that you have the power to change them.

VERSE 10

Therefore, the man who seeks his own welfare, should pull out this arrow—this arrow of lamentation, pain, and sorrow.

Negative emotions will not leave on their own. It is up to us to draw their poison our of our hearts.

VERSE 11

Speak or act with an impure mind,
And trouble will follow you.

When we speak or act insincerely, we open the door to trouble.

VERSE 12

Fine words bear fruit in a man who acts well in accordance with them.

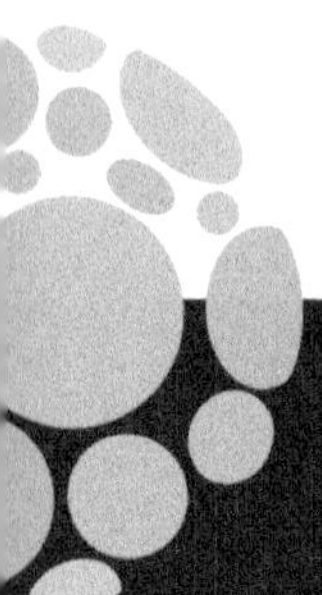

Making resolutions is good, but we need to follow our promises up with action.

VERSE 13

In making efforts to overcome wrong action, and to arouse right action, one practices Right Effort

We can't always be perfect, but if we are constantly trying to improve with a sincere heart, then we are doing the best we can.

VERSE 14

Understand that the body is merely the foam of a wave, the shadow of a shadow

As solid as it feels, our bodies are not permanent. Our spirits are.

VERSE 15

Free from passion and desire, you have stripped the thorns from the stem.

If we strip away negative emotions, then the flower of our self will blossom.

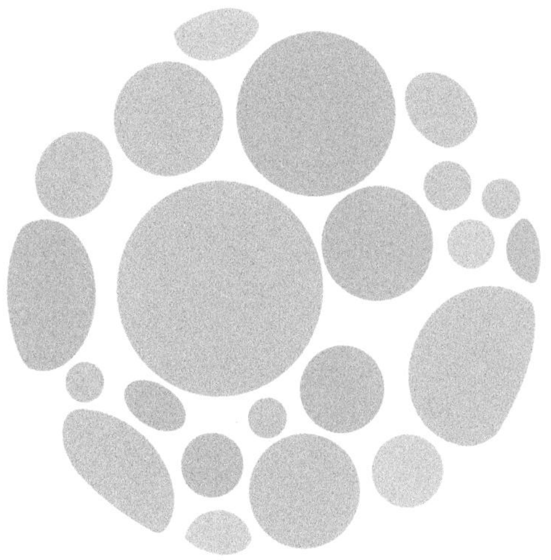

VERSE 16

Having torn one's fetters asunder, like a fish breaking a net in the water, not returning, like a fire not going back to what is already burned, one should wander solitary.

Find the strength to free yourself from unhealthy influences in your life.

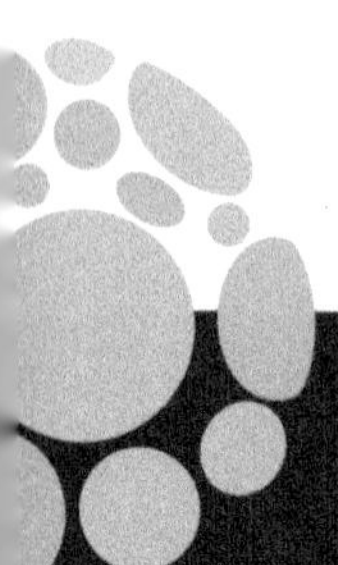

VERSE 17

By your own efforts waken yourself, watch yourself. And live joyfully. You are the master.

We are the masters of ourselves. It is up to us how we think, act, and live.

VERSE 18

However many holy words you read, However many you speak, What good will they do you If you do not act upon them?

Contemplating spiritual behaviors will not change your life. Acting on them will.

VERSE 19

Do what you have to do resolutely, with all your heart. The traveller who hesitates only raises dust on the road.

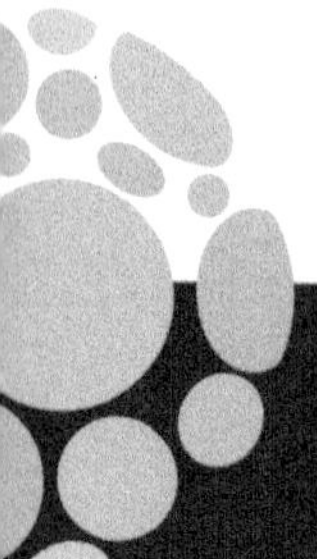

Never delay or hesitate before doing the right thing.

VERSE 20

All that we are arises with our thoughts.
With our thoughts we make the world.

Life can make you feel powerless. Learning how to think positively and look for opportunities to improve will help you take back your power.

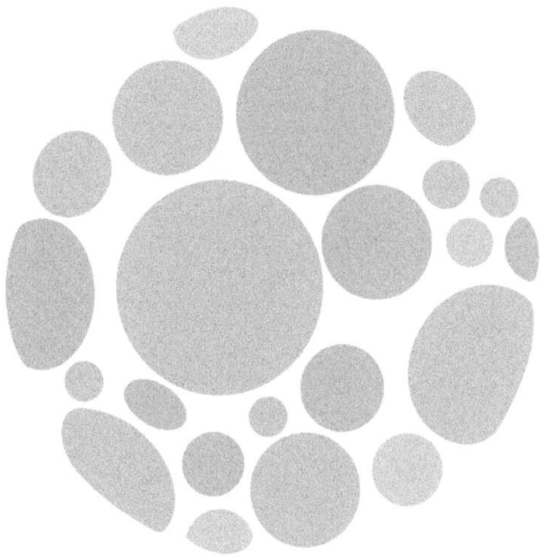

VERSE 21

Awake. Be the witness of your thoughts.

Don't dismiss any of your ideas. Even ones that seem bad might be the beginning of something good.

VERSE 22

But when he perceives the disappearance of the five hindrances in himself, it is as if he were freed from debt, from sickness, from bonds, from slavery, from the perils of the desert.

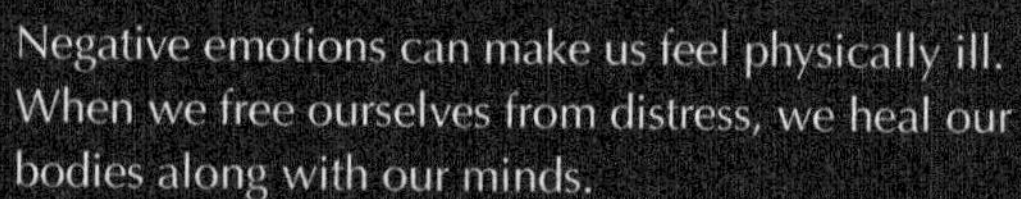

Negative emotions can make us feel physically ill. When we free ourselves from distress, we heal our bodies along with our minds.

VERSE 23

Let a wise man blow off the impurities of his self, as a smith blows off the impurities of silver one by one, little by little, and from time to time.

Becoming enlightened is not the work of a day. It is achieved in the small, steady steps we take every day.

VERSE 24

And how does one, in protecting others, protect oneself? By forbearance and nonviolence, by loving kindness and compassion. Thus in protecting others, one protects oneself.

Committing acts of violence, or even thinking hateful thoughts, are just as poisonous to us as to our enemy. Forgiveness is the healthy choice.

HAPPINESS

VERSE 25

There is happiness in life, happiness in friendship, happiness of a family, happiness in a healthy body and mind, but when one loses them, there is suffering.

It is easy to take the small blessings of life for granted. Happiness comes from remembering to be thankful for what we have.

VERSE 26

He who is earnest and meditative obtains ample joy.

Happiness isn't found. It is felt. We know happiness when we reflect on the honest good around us.

VERSE 27

If a man speaks or acts with a pure thought, happiness follows him, like a shadow that never leaves him.

Happiness comes to us when we do good things without ulterior motives.

VERSE 28

Happiness or sorrow: whatever befalls you, walk on untouched, unattached.

Do not gloat in victory or sulk in defeat. Go through life with a gracious heart.

VERSE 29

Give thanks for what had been given to you, however little. Be pure, never falter.

Regrets weigh you down. Enjoy the good, release the bad, and allow yourself to move on.

VERSE 30

It is in the nature of things that joy arises in a person free from remorse.

If we live without regrets, then happiness is sure to follow.

VERSE 31

Whether touched by happiness or sorrow, wise people are never depressed.

Dwelling on negativity—real or imagined—damages us. Find some joy in every day to restore happiness and tranquility.

VERSE 32

There is pleasure and there is bliss. Forgo the first to possess the second.

Physical pleasure is fleeting and unsatisfying. Spiritual bliss is lasting happiness.

VERSE 33

For a while the fool's mischief tastes sweet, sweet as honey. But in the end it turns bitter. And how bitterly he suffers!

Doing something bad can feel good in the moment, but sooner or later it always comes back to harm us.

VERSE 34

Can there be joy and laughter
When always the world
is ablaze? Enshrouded in
darkness Should you not seek
a light?

Even though the world can seem a dark place, we can choose to create happiness for ourselves and others.

VERSE 35

Just as water cools both good and bad and washes away all impurity and dust, in the same way you should develop thoughts of love.

Feeling love is good for us, so we should always be looking for people to share it.

VERSE 36

Pleasant feeling is impermanent, conditioned, dependently-arisen, bound to decay, to vanish, to fade away, to cease—and so too are painful feeling and neutral feeling.

Our feelings, good and bad, can change quickly. Things may get worse, but there is always hope that things can get better.

VERSE 37

Why do what you will regret? Why bring tears upon yourself? Do only what you do not regret, and fill yourself with joy.

Winning what we desire through wrongdoing will rob us of the joy of success.

VERSE 38

If by leaving a small pleasure one sees a great pleasure, let a wise man leave the small pleasure, and look to the great.

Lasting happiness doesn't come from material things or fleeting pleasures. Lasting happiness comes from living a life we can be proud of.

VERSE 39

There is no fire like passion,
there is no shark like hatred,
there is no snare like folly,
there is no torrent like greed.

Negative emotions are particularly harmful because they are strong and can overwhelm us with their poison.

VERSE 40

Fresh milk takes time to sour. So a fool's mischief takes time to catch up with him.

In the short term, wrongdoing may seem to pay off. But time will turn it sour.

VERSE 41

Nothing tends toward loss as does an untamed heart. The untamed heart tends towards loss. Nothing tends toward growth as does a tamed heart. The tamed heart tends towards growth.

We aren't perfect. We can make ourselves unhappy. But we should rejoice because there is always a chance to improve.

VERSE 42

Righteousness when well practised brings happiness.

Doing the right thing for its own sake—without expecting reward or praise—brings true happiness.

VERSE 43

Cherish the road of peace.

Peace is precious, and must be kept safe in our hearts, minds, and actions so that it may bring happiness into the world.

VERSE 44

The virtuous man delights in this world, and he delights in the next; he delights in both. He delights and rejoices, when he sees the purity of his own work.

Virtuousness comes from deriving real happiness from doing good works.

VERSE 45

I gladden my mind, fill it with joy, and make it immovable and unshakable.

Embrace your happiness, be grateful for it, and it cannot be taken from you.

VERSE 46

Nothing brings joy as does a tamed, controlled, attended and restrained heart. This heart brings joy.

Everything we need for happiness is inside us as long as we learn how to be content and virtuous.

VERSE 47

Know for yourselves: These are wholesome; these things are not blameworthy; these things are praised by the wise; undertaken and observed, these things lead to benefit and happiness, having undertaken them, abide in them.

We must learn how to find happiness through living well and identifying what is healthy.

VERSE 48

How happy he is following the path of the awakened.

Living and acting mindfully makes life a joyful journey.

VIRTUE

VERSE 49

In all the world,
every world,
you should do no evil
with speech,
body,
or mind.

There is no time, place, or reason that makes wrongdoing acceptable.

VERSE 50

The perfume of virtue travels against the wind and reaches into the ends of the world.

Virtue speaks for itself. If you do good works, the world can't help but notice.

VERSE 51

He whose evil deeds are covered by good deeds, brightens up this world, like the moon when freed from clouds.

We can't avoid making mistakes, but we can strive to outnumber our bad deeds with good ones.

VERSE 52

Let no one work another one's undoing
Or even slight him at all anywhere

Revenge, great or small, is petty and unsatisfying.

VERSE 53

Be quick to do good. If you are slow, the mind, delighting in mischief, will catch you.

Do not put off doing the right thing. Your delay will only leave room for misfortune down the line.

VERSE 54

The evil done by oneself, self-begotten, self-bred, crushes the foolish, as a diamond breaks a precious stone.

Hurting others doesn't make us feel better about ourselves. In fact, it creates even more poisonous, negative feelings in us.

VERSE 55

Let no man think lightly of good, saying in his heart, It will not come nigh unto me. Even by the falling of water-drops a water-pot is filled; the wise man becomes full of good, even if he gather it little by little.

We must learn to be grateful for the small blessings. They add up to make our lives good.

VERSE 56

Never let them wish each other ill through provocation or resentful thought.

We cannot be everyone's friend, but we can be no one's enemy.

VERSE 57

Quietly consider what is right and wrong. Receiving all opinions equally, without haste, wisely observe the law.

Listen to everyone's point of view before passing judgment.

VERSE 58

Be quiet and loving and fearless.

We must listen more than we speak, love instead of hate, and be brave in the face of challenges.

VERSE 59

Good people shine from afar, like the snowy mountains; bad people are not seen, like arrows shot by night.

While the evil in our lives is easy to brush off and forget, good people leave lasting, positive impressions on everyone they meet.

VERSE 60

If the traveler can find a virtuous and wise companion, let him go with him joyfully and overcome the dangers of the way.

Living the virtuous life is easier with supportive friends.

VERSE 61

Abandoning idle chatter, he speaks at the right time, what is correct and to the point, of Dhamma and discipline.

Avoid using words for bad purposes like lying or gossip. Spread positive, useful language into the world.

VERSE 62

The friend who is a helpmate, the friend in happiness and woe, the friend who gives good counsel, the friend who sympathizes too - these four as friends the wise behold and cherish them devotedly as does a mother her own child.

Find—and be—the kind of friend that stands true through thick and thin.

VERSE 63

Filled with infinite kindness, complete and well-developed; any limited actions one may have done do not remain lingering in one s mind.

Obsessing over your mistakes is a kind of selfishness. If you are too busy thinking about others, then you will not have time to be negative about yourself.

VERSE 64

And he who lives a hundred years, ignorant and unrestrained, a life of one day is better if a man is wise and reflecting.

The value of our time on earth comes from our actions rather than the number of our years.

VERSE 65

Do not speak harshly to anybody; Angry speech is painful, blows for blows will touch thee.

Think before you speak. Physical hurts heal, but wounds left by words can last a lifetime.

VERSE 66

Look not for recognition, but follow the awakened. And set yourself free.

Fame is fleeting. Find satisfaction in knowing you did the right thing even if no one else ever knows.

VERSE 67

You are the lamp to lighten the way. Then hurry, hurry.

Do not hold back the light of goodness. Let it shine through you.

VERSE 68

Life is hard for the man who quietly undertakes the way of perfection with purity, detachment, and vigor.

Being virtuous is difficult, and can feel like a sacrifice, but will be worth it in the end.

VERSE 69

Knowing that the other person is angry, one who remains mindful and calm acts for his own best interest and for the other's interest, too.

Responding to anger with anger escalates problems. Find the strength to remain calm in the face of rage.

VERSE 70

The disciple will find out the plainly shown path of virtue, as a clever man finds out the right flower.

Your conscience will tell you when you are doing right and wrong. Be sure to listen to what it says.

VERSE 71

Can you hide from your own mischief? Not in the sky, not in the midst of the ocean, nor deep in the mountains. Nowhere.

We cannot run from our mistakes. It is better to own them and make amends.

VERSE 72

Well-makers lead the water; fletchers bend the arrow; carpenters bend a log of wood; good people fashion themselves.

Good people are made, not born. There is always time to work on becoming a good person.

TRUTH

VERSE 74

When seeing your own nature it is necessary to see it at the very moment of speaking. One who does that perceives as does one who wields a sword in the height of battle.

Think before you speak. We often reveal who we are in the kind of words we choose to use.

VERSE 75

The wise person drives out heedlessness with heedfulness, having climbed the high tower of discernment.

Don't let fear rule you. Calm your panic and slow down. Clarity will give you perspective.

VERSE 76

In every trial, let understanding fight for you.

Try to keep your mind impartial and know when your imagination is running away with you.

VERSE 77

Your worst enemy cannot harm you as much as your own thoughts, unguarded. But once mastered, no one can help you as much, not even your father or your mother.

Our minds can turn against us, replaying bad memories, thoughts, and emotions. But if we control them, they give us the power to find good in anything.

VERSE 78

Men, driven by fear, go to many a refuge, to mountains and forests, to groves and sacred trees. But that is not a safe refuge, that is not the best refuge; a man is not delivered from all pains after having gone to that refuge.

Running away from problems means you will live in fear of them forever. Facing them gives you the chance to conquer your fear.

VERSE 79

By watching and working, the master makes for himself an island, which the flood cannot overwhelm.

Life can seem overwhelming, but by fortifying our minds and spirits we build a protection that can't be broken.

VERSE 80

Few are there among men who arrive at the other shore; the other people here run up and down the shore.

: It is not enough to identify the right path. We must find the courage to take it.

VERSE 81

In one truth is all truth and the ten thousand states are of themselves 'thus,' as they are.

When a problem seems complicated, take a deep breath. The solution may be simpler than you realize.

VERSE 82

See the false as false, the true as true. Look into your heart. Follow your nature.

Wisdom can also come from intuition. Listen to yours when it speaks.

VERSE 83

The wise man tells you where you have fallen and where you yet may fall – Invaluable secrets!

Be open to the wisdom of your teachers. They will help you avoid making mistakes.

VERSE 84

Do not follow the evil law! Do not live on in thoughtlessness! Do not follow false doctrine! Be not a friend of the world.

Do not blindly follow what you are told. Consult your sense of right and wrong.

VERSE 85

Let him resolve upon this mindfulness: This is Divine Abiding here, they say.

Living in the pursuit of truth moves us closer to the Divine.

VERSE 86

How can a troubled mind understand the way? If a man is disturbed, he will never be filled with knowledge.

We must learn to let go of our fears, concerns, and distractions. They impede our ability to learn from the present and move forward.

VERSE 87

Develop your concentration: for he who has concentration understands things according to their reality.

Being completely focused on our lives and in our meditations helps us understand them better.

VERSE 88

The master finds freedom from desire and sorrow - Freedom without bounds.

When we stop allowing our negative emotions to hold us back, we are able to see the world in new, exciting ways.

VERSE 89

Do not look for bad company or live with men who do not care. Find friends who love the truth.

Choose friends who are engaged with learning the truth instead of indifferent to it.

VERSE 90

Master your words. Let them serve truth.

Be careful of speaking carelessly. Say what you mean, and strive to speak only the truth.

VERSE 91

The wise have mastered body, word, and mind. They are the true masters.

Wisdom is not just knowing things. It's having the skill to control yourself.

VERSE 92

Do not carry with you your mistakes. Do not carry your cares. Travel alone like an elephant in the forest.

Focusing on worries and sorrows will not make them go away. Keep your focus on the present.

VERSE 93

So was my past existence at that time real, but unreal the future and present existence; and my future existence will be at one time real, but unreal the past and present existence; and my present existence is now real, but unreal the past and future existence.

Whoever we have been in the past and whoever we may be in the future is beyond our control. We can only decide who we want to be right now.

VERSE 94

Wisdom is purified by morality, and morality is purified by wisdom: where one is, the other is.

It is not enough to be knowledgable. We must develop the instinct to use that knowledge for the benefit of ourselves and others.

VERSE 95

No one saves us but ourselves, no one can and no one may.

While we may love others, we must learn to be accountable for our actions and feelings. We are responsible for our lives.

VERSE 96

The greatest impurity is ignorance. Free yourself from it. Be pure.

Ignorance breeds lies and hate. Knowledge leads to understanding and acceptance.

VERSE 97

In overcoming wrong action with attentive mind, and dwelling with attentive mind in possession of right action, one practices Right Attentiveness.

We must examine our actions to be sure that they are coming from good motives instead of bad ones.

ETERNITY

VERSE 98

All day long you seek fields of blessings only; you do not try to get out of the bitter sea of birth and death. If you are confused about your self-nature, how can blessings save you?

Before we can benefit from outside blessings, we must make ourselves worthy of them.

VERSE 99

Give up the old ways - Passion, enmity, folly. Know the truth and find peace.

When we refuse to harbor negative emotions, then we achieve lasting inner peace.

VERSE 100

To share happiness and to have done something good before leaving this life is sweet.

Living only for yourself is not as fulfilling as sharing your life and love with others.

VERSE 101

Open are the doors to the Deathless to those with ears. Let them show their conviction.

Being receptive to the wisdom of the world allows us to go confidently toward eternity.

VERSE 102

When one understands
that corporeality, feeling,
perception, mental formation,
and consciousness, are
transient, also in that case one
possesses Right Understanding.

All things pass away in time, so do not dwell on the evil and appreciate the good.

VERSE 103

When one sees it thus as it actually is with proper wisdom, one becomes disenchanted with the earth element and makes the mind dispassionate towards the earth element.

We must learn that material goods cannot give us lasting happiness and aren't as precious as the valued treasures of the soul.

VERSE 104

Faith is the best wealth for a man in this world.

Unlike material wealth, faith will bring lasting rewards beyond this life.

VERSE 105

The extinction of greed, the extinction of anger, the extinction of delusion: this, indeed, is called Nirvana.

We can be blinded by our negative emotions. When we push them away, we free our minds and create lasting peace.

VERSE 106

Long is the night to him who is awake; long is a mile to him who is tired; long is life to the foolish who do not know the true law.

The idea of Eternity is only scary if we do not surround ourselves willingly with virtue.

VERSE 107

This is deathless, the liberation of the mind through lack of clinging.

We make death upsetting when we root ourselves in attachment. If we can open our hearts to letting go of ourselves and others, then we may find peace.

VERSE 108

In a world become blind, I beat the drum of the Deathless.

Do not fear death. Embrace the blessings of Eternity with joy.

VERSE 109

You too shall pass away. Knowing this, how can you quarrel? How easily the wind overturns a frail tree.

When we remember that life is short, we realize that fighting is a waste of time.

VERSE 110

Even death is not to be feared by one who has lived wisely.

We fear the unknown after death. Going armed with the knowledge of virtue will make us brave.

VERSE 111

For great is the harvest in this world, and greater still in the next.

Performing good works benefits us in this life, but our true reward comes in the afterlife.

VERSE 112

Cross over to the father shore, beyond life and death. Do your thoughts trouble you? Does passion disturb you?

Remember not to let troubles burden you. They will have no hold on you after this life.

VERSE 113

When you have understood the destruction of all that was made, you will understand that which was not made.

Once we accept that the material will fall apart, we realize what is spiritual, permanent, and valuable.

VERSE 114

Wakefulness is the way to life. The fool sleeps as if he were already dead, but the master is awake and he lives forever.

They who are alert to the spiritual path need not fear death, as their spirits will out live their bodies.

VERSE 115

There is no suffering for him who has finished his journey, and abandoned grief, who has freed himself on all sides, and thrown off all fetters.

Rather than fearing death, rejoice in the knowledge that human pain and suffering does not follow.

VERSE 116

Better than a hundred years of mischief is one day spent in contemplation.

Time spent thinking is never wasted. Consider before acting in haste.

VERSE 117

Yielding like the earth, Joyous and clear like the lake, Still as the stone at the door, He is free from life and death.

By maintaining a peaceful balance in our hearts and minds, we will have nothing to fear from life or death.

VERSE 118

Let go of anger. Let go of pride. When you are bound by nothing you go beyond sorrow.

Life is short, and we should not spend it as a prisoner to our own negativity.

VERSE 119

And he who lives a hundred years, not seeing the immortal place, a life of one day is better if a man sees the immortal place.

The life spent in pursuit of spirituality, no matter how long, is the most worthy.

VERSE 120

Free yourself from attachment. Know the sweet joy of the way.

Do not tie yourself down to the impermanent world. Focus on the eternal joys that come from the spiritual path.

VERSE 121

When your light shines without impurity or desire, you will come into the boundless country.

When your spirit is cleansed of negative emotions and experiences, then you will arrive in a spiritual state.

CREDITS

All Photos from Shutterstock

Cover: Andrew Rafalsky,
Gita Kulinitch Studio

p. 10: DUSAN ZIDAR
p. 12: Anna Andersson Fotografi
p. 13: MaxyM
p. 14: vvvita
p. 15: vvvita
p. 16: Karen Faljyan
p. 18: vvvita
p. 19: vvvita
p. 20: vvvita
p. 21: Renata Apanaviciene
p. 22: vvvita
p. 24: vvvita
p. 25: vvvita
p. 26: vvvita
p. 27: vvvita
p. 28: vvvita
p. 30: Roman Pyshchyk
p. 31: Roman Pyshchyk
p. 32: Roman Pyshchyk
p. 33: vvvita
p. 34: vvvita
p. 36: vvvita
p. 37: vvvita
p. 38: ANURAK PONGPATIMET
p. 42: vvvita
p. 43: vvvita
p. 44: vvvita
p. 45: pasSsy
p. 46: Adi Burca
p. 48: vvvita
p. 49: Konstanttin
p. 50: Roman Pyshchyk
p. 51: vvvita
p. 52: Roman Pyshchyk
p. 54: vvvita
p. 55: Smit
p. 56: kryzhov
p. 57: vvvita
p. 58: vvvita
p. 60: Im stocker
p. 61: yari2000
p. 62: vvvita
p. 63: Ronnachai Palas
p. 64: Ekaterina Iatcenko
p. 66: Chepko Danil Vitalevich
p. 67: Dora Zett
p. 68: Kokosha Yuliya
p. 69: slonme
p. 72: piyapong tulachom
p. 74: Poprotskiy Alexey
p. 75: vvvita
p. 76: vvvita
p. 78: vvvita
p. 79: Vaclav Volrab
p. 80: Dmytro Buianskyi
p. 81: piyapong tulachom
p. 82: Gelpi
p. 84: Roman Pyshchyk
p. 85: vvvita

p. 86: Roman Pyshchyk
p. 87: Roman Pyshchyk
p. 88: Ivan Marjanovic
p. 90: vvvita
p. 91: vvvita
p. 92: vvvita
p. 93: Sucharn Wetthayasapha
p. 94: ANUCHA PONGPATIMETH
p. 96: 5 second Studio
p. 97: Branka Tasevski
p. 98: Maksim Mazur
p. 99: iproname
p. 100: vvvita
p. 104: DenisNata
p. 105: vvvita
p. 106: Mysikrysa
p. 107: vvvita
p. 108: ANUCHA PONGPATIMETH
p. 110: tatyana trofimova
p. 111: ANUCHA PONGPATIMETH
p. 112: ANUCHA PONGPATIMETH
p. 113: DavidTB
p. 114: Pitipat Usanakornkul
p. 116: ANUCHA PONGPATIMETH
p. 117: Peyker
p. 118: Tania Pishchana
p. 119: hwongcc
p. 120: Anastasija Popova
p. 122: Lucky Business
p. 123: Kuttelvaserova Stuchelova
p. 124: Rita Kochmarjova
p. 125: iproname
p. 126: Photo-SD
p. 128: Canon Boy
p. 129: Rita Kochmarjova
p. 130: Alena Ozerova
p. 131: vvvita
p. 134: Lapina
p. 135: Chekky
p. 136: Natalya Rozhkova
p. 137: MaraZe
p. 138: otsphoto
p. 140: Anna Vangorodska
p. 141: vvvita
p. 142: Milkos
p. 143: Volodymyr Burdiak
p. 144: Roman Pyshchyk
p. 146: Volodymyr Burdiak
p. 147: oley
p. 148: schankz
p. 149: scigelova
p. 150: Roman Pyshchyk
p. 152: ryabuha kateryna
p. 153: Sheila Fitzgerald
p. 154: Forrest Keel
p. 155: Big Pack Stock
p. 156: DenisNata
p. 158: Tania Pishchana
p. 159: Hannah Skalova
p. 160: otsphoto
p. 161: Aleksei Ruzhin

CPSIA information can be obtained
at www.ICGtesting.com
Printed in the USA
BVOW11s0530271217
503489BV00009B/31/P

9 781633 535237